Pterosaurs
The Flying Reptiles

Dinosaur Books For Young Readers
By
Enrique Fiesta

Mendon Cottage Books

JD-Biz Publishing

Download Free Books!
http://MendonCottageBooks.com

Read More Amazing Animal Books

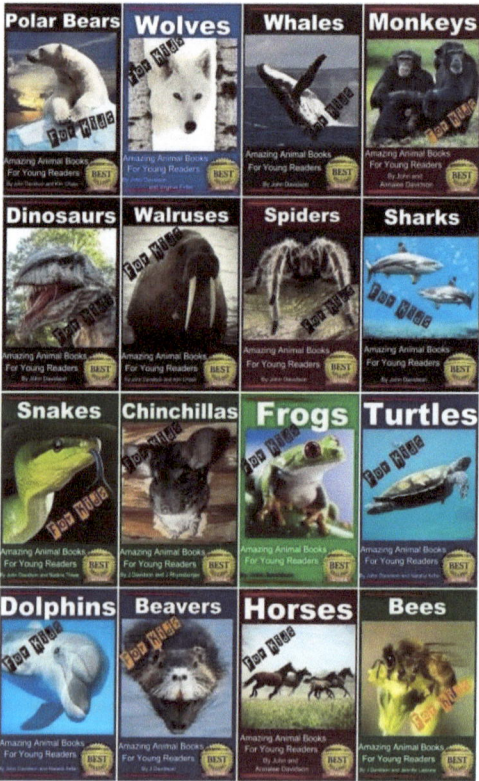

Purchase at Amazon.com

Download Free Books!
http://MendonCottageBooks.com

Table of Contents

Introduction

Salutations young reader! Today we are going to take a step back in time and enter the age of the dinosaurs. The dinosaurs are an extinct species of animal that began to live on the Earth over 200 million years ago. "Extinct" means that they no longer exist.

The dinosaurs are some of the most intriguing and awe-inspiring animals that have existed on our planet. The dinosaurs' colossal size, strange characteristics, and mysterious disappearance make them *inherently* worthy of study and interest. Even more than these reasons, the study of dinosaurs itself is an incredible adventure which requires thought and imagination. The study of dinosaurs helps you to appreciate just how mysterious life really is. Our planet supports not only us and the animals that live today, but it even supported creatures as gigantic and strange as the dinosaurs- just think how cool that is! I hope that you bring a spirit of openness and wonder to your reading, and that you come to appreciate the mystery and value of the dinosaurs.

In this book we are going to learn about the Pterosaurs! The Pterosaurs were winged, flying reptiles which lived during the age of the dinosaurs. The pterosaurs are not considered dinosaurs by scientists, but reptiles. We are going to learn about these winged creatures, where and when they lived, and their relationship with the creatures they lived with. The pterosaurs are often mistakenly called "pterodactyls" but the *Pterodactyl* is actually just a species of Pterosaur. The Pterosaurs included many species of flying reptiles which ranged considerably in size; from the size of a sparrow to the size of an airplane.

We know what we know about the dinosaurs from a variety of sources including fossils, biology, and other scientific disciplines. Fossils are the ancient remains of the dinosaurs, the most familiar being their bones. Biological science is the study of life in general, but many scientists compare the dinosaurs to modern day animals to support their theories.

Before a talk about dinosaurs can take place it is important that we discuss the theory of evolution. Evolutionary theory supposes that all the animals we know and see today are the direct descendants of animals that existed millions of years ago. The dinosaurs and other creatures that existed millions of years ago either died out or gradually changed into different animals. For instance, birds are considered to be surviving dinosaurs because their dinosaur ancestors survived the dinosaur extinction event (we will discuss this later). The pterosaurs are more closely related to birds than any other reptile.

Remember that any time you see an * next to the name of a dinosaur, it means that a book has been written about this dinosaur in the Dinosaur Books for Young Readers series. Any word written in bold is an important scientific term which is defined in-text. Italics are used to denote the first time a dinosaur's name is mentioned in the book.

Chapter 1: Appearance

The Pterosaurs were interesting reptiles because they came in all shapes and sizes, though they shared many similarities. Pterosaurs typically had long jaws filled with needle-like teeth; others possessed more beak-like mouths with no teeth.

The Pterosaurs possessed leathery wings. The wings were made up of unique membranes that were attached to a very long finger, the sides of the Pterosaur, and the ankles of the Pterosaur. The Pterosaur possessed a **wishbone**. The wishbone is a forked bone in animals that typically serves as an attachment point for powerful muscles. It is found in birds, where it serves as an attachment point for the wing muscles. It served the same purpose for Pterosaurs. The Pterosaur was capable of powered flight because of its leathery wings. Another factor which aided the Pterosaur to fly was its hollow bones. The presence of hollow bones means that the Pterosaurs were lighter than dinosaurs of roughly the same size which have solid bones; when flying the Pterosaur would have had less weight to carry around.

Most Pterosaurs possessed webbed-feet. Webbed feet also an animal to walk on mud or swim with more ease than animals without the characteristic; such webbing makes sense for a Pterosaur to have since they lived in primarily aquatic environments (see Chapter 3).

Pterosaurs shared a number of characteristics including their wings, elongated jaws, and wishbone, but their skulls varied immensely. The **crests** of Pterosaurs came in unique shapes and sizes. A crest on a Pterosaur refers to the tuft of skin on a Pterosaur's head. The *Pteranodon* possessed a back-ward facing spike like crest whereas the *Tapejarids* possessed elaborate fan-like crests. The crests were generally composed entirely of tissue which does not fossilize. This means that scientists have difficulty reconstructing what Pterosaurs looked like because they do not have access to fossilized crests.

The Pterosaurs were probably a shade of tan, brown, or green like most animals. These earthy colors would have given the Pterosaur **camouflage.** Camouflage is the natural ability of an animal to blend into its surroundings. It is possible that the crests of the Pterosaurs were vibrant, bright colors. Many birds have colorful crests, and though it might have meant less camouflage the Pterosaur might not have needed it due to its ability to fly away quickly if danger arose.

Chapter 2: Behavior

The Pterosaurs were **predators**, specifically **piscavorous predators**. A piscavorous predator is an animal that eats fish to survive. The Pterosaurs were also likely to have been **scavengers**. A scavenger is an animal that eats from carcasses, namely the remains of animal that the scavenging animal did not kill. In addition to carcasses and fish, their diet was supplemented by small reptiles and insects.

The Pterosaurs used their power of flight to assist them when they hunted. They likely would fly above the ocean and swoop down to capture fish prey. The Pterosaurs had a powerful vision which allowed them to see fish under water, much like hawks and ospreys today.

Even though the Pterosaurs could fly they had to be aware of their surroundings; this is because Pterosaurs could become prey for **therapods**. Therapods were predatory, bipedal (walked on two legs) dinosaurs which typically had sharp claws and teeth. There are fossilized remains of a *Spinosaurus** tooth embedded in a Pterosaur spinal bones. The Spinosaurus likely waited underwater for the Pterosaur to soar down to the surface of the water before thrusting out of the water and chomping down on the surprised Pterosaur.

Pterosaurs laid eggs like birds and the dinosaurs. It is probable that they buried their eggs, like modern day crocodiles. The Pterosaurs did not take care of their young when they hatched (like birds and crocodilians) because they were able to fly shortly after they hatched.

Chapter 3: Environment

The Pterosaurs, like all dinosaurs, lived during the **Mesozoic Era**. The Mesozoic Era began about 250 million years ago and ended about 60 million years ago. The Mesozoic Era is divided into three periods: the **Triassic, Jurassic,** and **Cretaceous**. The climate of the era was considerably warmer and more humid than it is today. There were wet, dry, and arid environments but all of them were typically very warm. There were no polar ice caps during the age of the dinosaurs; also, all of the continents were much closer together than they are today. Most of the dinosaurs we are familiar with lived during the Jurassic and the Cretaceous, though the ancestors of the more popular dinosaurs have their origins in the Triassic Period. The era of the dinosaurs ended at the end of the Cretaceous Period during what is called the **K-Pg extinction event**. After this event almost every single dinosaur species became extinct. The extinction of the dinosaurs was probably caused by a combination of events including disease, meteoric impacts, and climate change.

The Pterosaurs have their origins in the Late Triassic Period and survived until the K-Pg extinction event (228 million years ago to 66 million years ago). The Pterosaurs have been discovered all over the globe including North America, Europe, Australia, and Africa. The Pterosaurs most likely lived near water; such as coastal regions, lagoons, and fresh water environments. The Pterosaurs were also scavengers so it is likely that they would fly inland to eat when the occasion came up. The Pterosaurs lived within **bio-diverse** environments and for a large space of time- nearly 190 million years! Bio-diverse environments are those environs which house a large number of species of organisms. The Pterosaurs lived with a countless number of animals and dinosaurs, but we will learn about a few just. The Pterosaurs lived with the *Tyrannosaurus Rex**, the *Tylosaurus**, and the *Apatosaurus**. There are books in the Dinosaur Books for Young Readers series for all three of these dinosaurs.

The Tyrannosaurus Rex is perhaps the most famous dinosaur in history owing to its fearsome name, reputation, and media attention. The Tyrannosaurus was a powerful predator of the Late Cretaceous and could grow as large as 40 ft. long and 20 ft. high. This dinosaur was powerful enough to take down the large herbivores it lived with.

Herbivores are animals that eat vegetation to survive. The Pterosaurs flew in the skies above the Tyrannosaur, but it is likely that the two reptiles would come into contact on occasion. Whenever there were dinosaur carcasses lying about the Pterosaurs would swoop in to scavenge the remains, as vultures do today. The Tyrannosaur was most likely also a scavenger and would have scared off the Pterosaurs to feed on the carcasses by itself. The Pterosaurs were far too small to pose any threat to a Tyrannosaur and so would have flown away or waited for the Tyrannosaur to leave.

The Tylosaurus was a Late Cretaceous beast of the sea. The Tylosaurus was the largest **mosasaur** to ever live. The mosasaurs were marine reptiles with paddle-like fins, elongated tails, and long jaws with sharp teeth. The Tylosaurus, like the Pterosaurs, fed mainly on fish and marine animals; however, it is quite possible that the Tylosaurus could leap out of the water to catch and eat Pterosaurs when they flew down to catch fish. Modern sharks do the same to birds so it is not implausible that Pterosaurs were food for Tylosaurus quick enough to catch the winged reptiles. Most Pterosaurs would have stood no chance against a full grown Tylosaurus since they could grow to a length of up to 50 ft. and a weigh as much as 7 tons.

The Apatosaurus was a **sauropod** which lived during the Jurassic Period. A sauropod is a dinosaur characterized by a long neck and tail, thick legs and torso, a small head, and powerful, trunk-like legs. The Apatosaurus fed mainly from the tops of trees, using its rake-like mouth to comb tree branches of their foliage. The Pterosaur and

Apatosaurus would have lived harmoniously because of their differing diets and because neither hunted the other. Small Pterosaurs might have perched on the Apatosaurus's back for protection and free travel much like modern birds do with regard to elephants.

Conclusion

We have taken a trip back in time to the age of the dinosaurs. We have learned about the Pterosaur, including what it looked like, its age and environment, and the dinosaurs it lived with. If we use our imaginations and knowledge we can engage and encounter the dinosaurs in all their mystery. When we appreciate the dinosaurs we come to appreciate the value of our own present age and all the wonderful creatures we know and love today. Through the study of dinosaurs we discover how diverse and wonderful nature really is. The animals we know today, we encounter with a newfound sense of wonder- and *wonder* is of the utmost importance in any study. So make sure that you keep thinking and learning and *really* make sure that you never lose your sense of wonder.

Author Bio

Enrique Fiesta

I was born in Southwest Florida and I hold a degree in Latin and Greek language and literature. In addition to my principal studies, I have also studied philosophy, history, the natural sciences, and literature. In my spare time I devote the vast majority of my time to reading, writing, praying, and walking. I am currently pursuing legal studies in order to become an attorney. After I earn my law degree I intend to pursue a doctorate in philosophy, literature, and politics.

Our books are available at

1. Amazon.com

2. Barnes and Noble

3. Itunes

4. Kobo

5. Smashwords

6. Google Play Books

Download Free Books!
http://MendonCottageBooks.com

Publisher

JD-Biz Corp

P O Box 374

Mendon, Utah 84325

http://www.jd-biz.com/

![Mendon Cottage Books]